To Auset Sophia Jones,
with all my love!

You were born powerful! Whatever you want is yours. Wherever your imagination takes you is possible!

You are WHOLE,

PERFECT

STRONG,

LOVING,

and

HARMONIOUS!

You are whole, perfect, strong, loving, and harmonious!

You were born with a wonderful gift! This gift makes it possible for you to accomplish whatever you can imagine. Would you like to know how I work?

I am the part of the mind called the subconscious. I'm always working. I'm the magic part that CREATES what you imagine! To understand me better please call me "the soil".

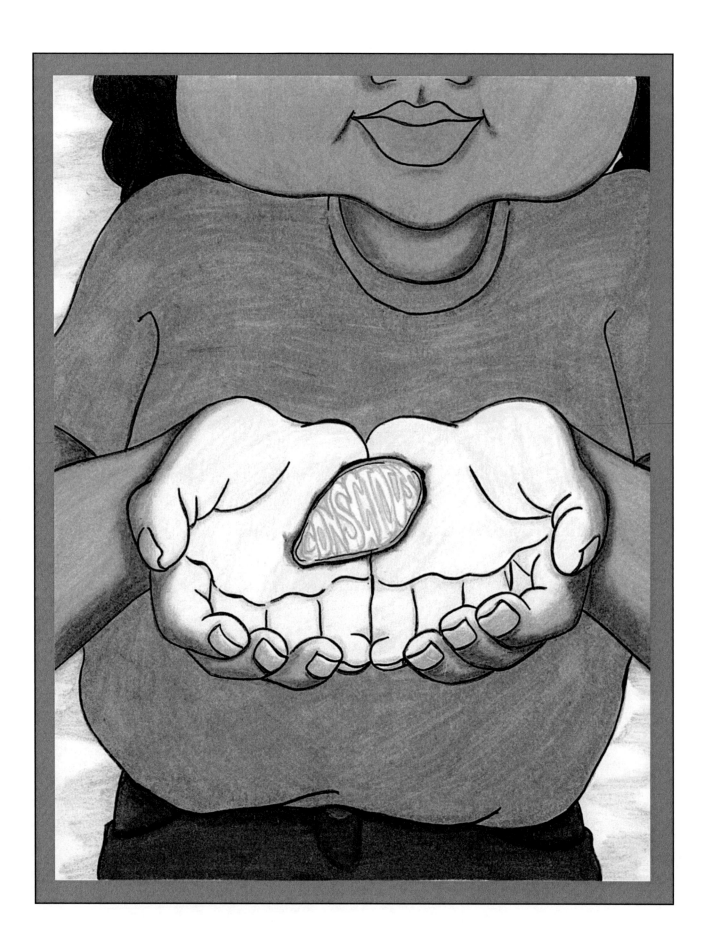

I work with the other part of the mind called the conscious to make you powerful. We'll call the conscious mind "the seed".

Let's take a pumpkin seed and plant the seed into the soil. (Remember the soil is your subconscious mind).

Once the pumpkin seeds are firmly and safely planted into the soil; pat the soil into place and walk away.

What do you expect to see sprout in the coming weeks?

An apple tree?

Orange flowers?

A pumpkin patch?

See, once you plant the pumpkin seeds you can only expect a full pumpkin patch! It will be impossible for anything different to sprout!

Whatever thoughts (seeds) planted in the soil will certainly sprout. There is deep wisdom and knowing in the soil. There is no need to worry, there is no need to guess; only a knowing and an expectation.

Simply plant, water, then walk away!

Whatever you choose to plant is what the soil will honor. Whatever you choose to plant will grow.

Remember, we are all born with the soil. You get to choose what seeds to plant. So choose wisely and responsibly,

THE END

Fun Pages

Now that you have read the book let's have some FUN!

On the next page DRAW and COLOR what seeds you are planting or would like to plant.

Now, let's draw and color in a picture of yourself along with the seeds you would like to plant or are planting.

About the Author

"The Soil is Good" is Tori Johnson-Jones' first children's book. Her passion to become an author was born following the birth of her daughter, Auset Sophia. A lifelong lover of books that taught about the boundless power of the mind and human potential, Tori lamented there was such a small genre for children. In the spirit of all she learned in her readings, Tori put pen to paper and created the work you now hold in your hand. Prior to becoming an author, Tori travelled the world as a celebrity makeup artist, working with clients such as Destiny's Child and Outkast. In all, she worked professionally for more than 15 years in the music business, even going on to become a successful singer/songwriter and performer. Tori is the founder of LoudSilence Music Group as well the popular lifestyle blog 'Music.Life.Lipstick & Coffee.' Tori is also working on her empowerment series 'Women & Wisdom: Stories to Empower our Girls' and the powerful documentary 'Mommy, Interrupted', a stirring saga celebrating her journey in the long-awaited birth of a child after a heart wrenching period of devastating loss. Feeling a strong calling upon her life, Tori prays "The Soil is Good" and her future works will be received in the spirit of universal uplift for which they are intended. Tori Jones hails from Atlanta, Georgia and currently lives in Washington, D.C. with her husband and young daughter. To visit her blog, www.loudsilencebrand.com

Made in the USA
Middletown, DE
19 April 2016